A ROOKIE READER

WHERE IS IT?

By Dee Lillegard

Illustrations by Gene Sharp

Prepared under the direction of Robert Hillerich, Ph.D.

CHILDRENS PRESS ™

CHICAGO

Library of Congress Cataloging in Publication Data

Lillegard, Dee.
  Where is it?

  (A Rookie reader)
  Summary: A search for a red cap results in a
surprising ending.
  [1. Lost and found possessions—Fiction] I. Sharp,
Gene, 1923-   ill. II. Title.   III. Series.
PZ7.L6275Wh 1984   [E]   84-70C5
ISBN 0-516-02065-X

7 8 9 10 11 12 13 14 15 16 R 02 01 00 99 98 97 96 95 94

Where is it?
Not in here.

Not in this.

Not under there.

Not behind this.

Where?

Not here.

Not here.

Not there.

Where?

Maybe this.
No, not this.

Maybe that.

No, not that.

Up there?

Not up there.

Next to this?

Inside that?

Over there?

It's nowhere!

Look around.
Look around.

If I was a red cap,
where would I be found...

You!

"Goo!"

WORD LIST

			there
a	I	maybe	this
around	if	next	to
be	in	no	under
behind	inside	not	up
cap	is	nowhere	was
found	it	over	where
goo	it's	red	would
here	look	that	you

About the Author

Dee Lillegard is the author of over 200 published stories, poems, and puzzles for children, plus WORD SKILLS, an eight-book set of high-interest grammar worktexts. She is co-author of CRAZY LETTER FRIENDS, a reading readiness program published in California. Ms. Lillegard has also worked as a children's editor and has appeared on television and radio in the San Francisco-Bay Area as a dream analyst. Many of her story ideas have come from her dreams and from her own three children, who are now all bigger than she is.

About the Artist

Gene Sharp has illustrated books, including school books, for a number of publishers. Among the books he has illustrated for Childrens Press are *The Super Snoops and the Missing Sleepers, Too Many Balloons,* and several in the "That's a Good Question" series.